AMANDA OTIS

REVENUE RISE FOR RENTALS:

A Complete Guide to Growing Your Short-Term Rental Property Business

Revenue Rise for Rentals:

A Complete Guide to Growing Your Short-Term Rental Property Business

AMANDA OTIS

OTIS
PUBLISHING

Contents

Dedication

To all the dreamers, creators, and hosts who pour their hearts into crafting unforgettable stays—this book is for you.

My passion for design, photography, and creating exceptional guest experiences has fueled my journey in the short-term rental industry. I believe that every thoughtful detail, from a well-placed amenity to a beautifully captured listing photo, has the power to elevate a space, delight guests, and increase revenue in ways you never imagined.

Thank you for purchasing Revenue Rise for Rentals. I truly appreciate your trust in this guide, and I hope it inspires you to take your rental to new heights. May your bookings be plentiful, your guests be delighted, and your success continue to grow.

Wishing you all the best in your short-term rental journey!

Amanda

Chapter 1 Introduction: What is Short-Term Rental Hosting and Why is it Popular?

If you're looking for a way to earn extra income, short-term rental hosting is a great option to consider. Online platforms like Airbnb, VRBO, and others connect travelers with hosts willing to rent their homes or spare rooms. As a host, you can make money by renting out your space to guests who are looking for a comfortable and affordable alternative to hotels. Short-term rental sites like these have become the most popular way to stay due to their ability to provide travelers with unique and authentic experiences that they might not get from a traditional hotel stay.

These platforms are so popular among travelers because of the variety of available accommodations. Whether you're looking for a cozy apartment in the heart of the city or a spacious villa in the countryside, you'll find something that suits your needs and budget. Plus, many short-term rental listings come with amenities like a kitchen, laundry facilities, and free Wi-Fi, making your stay more comfortable and convenient.

For hosts, short-term rentals offer a flexible and lucrative way to earn extra income. By renting out your space, you can earn money to help pay your bills or save up for a big purchase. And because these platforms allow you to set your prices and availability, you can choose when and how often you want to host guests.

Of course, short-term rental hosting isn't without its challenges. As a host, you'll need to be prepared to deal with the logistics of managing your property, communicating with guests, and handling any issues that may arise. But with the right prepa- ration and mindset, hosting can be a rewarding and profitable experience.

In the rest of this guide, we'll provide you with everything you need to know to become a successful short-term rental host. From setting up your listing to managing your finances, we'll cover all the essential aspects of hosting on Airbnb and similar online platforms. So, whether you're a first-time host or an experienced pro, read on to discover how to make the most of your short-term vacation rental hosting experience.

Chapter 2 Getting Started: Creating a Short-term Rental Account and Listing Your Property

Before you can start hosting on Airbnb or a similar platform, you must create an account and list your property.

Choose Platforms

With so many short-term rental platforms available today, it's important to research and compare your options. While most offer similar fees and host protection, each platform has unique features that may better suit your specific needs. Taking the time to evaluate them can help you make the best choice for your rental.

Create Short-Term Rental Platform Accounts

To create a short-term rental account, go to the short-term rental website or download the short-term rental app from the Apple Store or Google Play. Click on "Sign up" and enter your email address, password, and full name. You may need to confirm your email address by clicking on a link from an email the website will send you.

Complete Your Profile

Once you've created an account, you must complete your profile. This includes uploading a profile photo, verifying your phone number, and providing some basic information about yourself. Completing your profile can help you build trust with potential guests and make them more likely to book your listing.

List Your Property

To list your property on a short-term rental website, click on "List Your Space" and follow the prompts to provide details about your space. You'll need to include information like the property type (e.g., house, apartment, or room), the number of guests it can accommodate, and the location. You'll also need to provide photos of your space to help potential guests understand what it looks like.

Set Your Price and Availability

After you've provided all the details about your space, you'll need to set your price and availability. Short-term rental sites offer a range of pricing options, including nightly, weekly, and monthly rates. You can also set minimum and maximum stays and adjust your prices based on the season or special events.

Review and Publish Your Listing

Once you've set your price and availability, review your listing to make sure everything looks correct. You can preview your listing to see how it will appear to potential guests. If you're happy with your listing, click on "Publish" to make it live on the short-term rental platform.

Congratulations, you've now created your first short-term vacation rental listing! Of course, creating a listing is just the first step. In the rest of this guide, we'll cover everything you need to know to make your listing stand out, attract guests, and provide them with a great experience.

Chapter 3 Setting Up Your Space: Creating a Guest-Ready Home

Once you've listed your short-term vacation rental property online, it's time to prepare it for guests. Here are some tips for creating a guest-ready home that will leave a great impression.

Clean and Declutter

Before welcoming your first guests, prepare your rental property meticulously to ensure it meets high cleanliness and organization standards. Begin by thoroughly dusting all surfaces, including hard-to-reach areas like ceiling fans, light fixtures, and baseboards. Vacuum and mop floors in every room, paying special attention to corners and under furniture. Sanitize frequently touched surfaces such as doorknobs, light switches, and remote controls. Remove all personal items, including family photos, clothing, or personal toiletries, to create a neutral and inviting space.

Double-check that closets, drawers, and cabinets are either empty or stocked with essentials intended for guest use. Finally, stage the space thoughtfully by arranging furniture, fluffing pillows, and ensuring any decor enhances the overall ambiance. A spotless and clutter-free home makes a lasting positive impression and contributes to a five-star guest experience.

Provide Essential Amenities

Ensure your short-term rental is fully stocked with all the essential amenities to provide a comfortable and seamless stay for your guests. Start with the basics for the bedroom: provide high-quality, clean linens, including fitted sheets, flat sheets, pillowcases, and extra blankets or comforters for each bed. Offer multiple towel sets per guest, including bath towels, hand towels, and washcloths. For the bathroom, stock it with toiletries such as soap, shampoo, conditioner, body wash, and lotion, as well as extras like a hairdryer, disposable razors, and cotton swabs.

In the kitchen, supply a comprehensive set of cookware, including pots, pans, baking sheets, and various cooking utensils. Make sure dishes, glassware, and silverware are available in quantities that match your maximum guest occupancy, along with essentials like a cutting board, knife set, and can opener. Include basic pantry items like salt, pepper, sugar, coffee, tea, and cooking oil, and ensure guests have access to a coffee maker, kettle, and toaster. Add thoughtful touches like paper towels, dish soap, sponges, and trash bags to make their stay hassle-free. Providing a well-equipped home ensures guests feel welcome and cared for, leading to positive reviews and repeat bookings.

Add Personal Touches

Enhance your guests' experience by adding thoughtful personal touches that make them feel truly welcome and valued. Begin with a warm and inviting atmosphere by placing fresh flowers or a small potted plant in the living room or dining area. Consider providing a personalized welcome basket tailored to your guests' preferences, containing items like snacks, bottled water, coffee, tea, local treats, or even a small bottle of wine. Include a handwritten welcome note to create a more personal connection.

You can also incorporate small yet impactful details, such as a stack of books or magazines for leisure reading, a selection of board games, or even a local music playlist. For guests traveling with children, add family-friendly touches like coloring books, toys, or a list of kid-friendly activities in the area. These thoughtful extras elevate their stay and increase the likelihood of glowing reviews and repeat bookings.

Check Your Wi-Fi and Technology

In today's highly connected world, offering reliable Wi-Fi and up-to-date technology is essential to meeting guest expectations and ensuring a positive experience. Start by ensuring your Wi-Fi connection is strong, fast, and reliable throughout the entire property, including common areas and bedrooms. If your space is large or has Wi-Fi dead zones, consider adding signal boosters or mesh network systems. Provide clear and easy-to-follow instructions for connecting to the network, along with the Wi-Fi name and password, ideally printed and displayed in a prominent location like the living room or kitchen.

For entertainment, equip your property with a modern television capable of streaming. Ensure the TV is set up with popular streaming services such as Netflix, Hulu, or Amazon Prime, and include instructions for accessing these platforms. If you offer subscription-based streaming accounts, log in and verify they are ready for guest use. Alternatively, provide clear steps for guests to log in with their own accounts, with a reminder to log out upon checkout.

Test all technology before guests arrive, including smart home devices like thermostats, smart speakers, or home security systems. Offer additional convenience by including a charging station with multiple ports or adapters for various devices, as well as backup batteries for remote controls. Thoughtful preparation in this area ensures guests can stay connected and entertained, making their stay more enjoyable and worry-free.

Create a Welcome Guide and Clear House Rules

Establishing clear and comprehensive house rules is essential to setting expectations and preventing misunderstandings during your guests' stay. Begin by outlining your policies regarding critical areas, such as noise levels. Specify quiet hours to respect neighbors, particularly if your property is in a shared building or residential area. Clearly state your smoking policy, whether smoking is prohibited entirely or allowed in designated outdoor areas. If your property allows pets, detail specific guidelines, such as leash requirements, cleaning responsibilities, or restricted areas within the home.

For added convenience and charm, create a detailed guidebook with local recommendations, including nearby restaurants, coffee shops, grocery stores, and popular attractions. Highlight unique experiences like local markets, hiking trails, or cultural events. Include practical information, such as Wi-Fi details, house rules, and emergency contacts.

Include rules about the use of amenities, such as the proper operation of appliances, swimming pools, or hot tubs. For properties with outdoor spaces, specify rules about barbecues, fire pits, or the disposal of trash. If your rental has a maximum occupancy limit, parking restrictions, or guidelines for hosting visitors, these should be clearly stated as well.

Communicate these rules effectively by including them in your booking confirmation email, listing platform, and a printed house manual provided onsite. Use a friendly yet professional tone to ensure guests feel guided rather than restricted. For added clarity, consider using bullet points or visuals for key rules. This proactive approach creates a smoother experience for your guests and helps protect your property and maintain positive relationships with neighbors and future renters.

Remember, providing a comfortable and welcoming space is key to getting positive reviews and repeat bookings. In the next chapter, we'll cover how to set the right price for your listing.

You can find hosting resources, tools, and customizable hosting templates online at Otis Design Boutique.

Chapter 4 Pricing Your Space: How to Set the Right Price for Your Listing

Setting the right price for your short-term rental listing can be a challenge. You want to make sure you're charging enough to cover your expenses and make a profit, but you don't want to price yourself out of the market. Here are some tips for pricing your space:

Research Your Competition

Conducting thorough research on your competition is a crucial step in determining the optimal pricing strategy for your short-term rental. Start by identifying other listings in your area that closely match your property in terms of size, location, and features. Focus on properties with similar bedrooms and bathrooms, comparable proximity to local attractions or transportation hubs, and similar amenities such as a pool, parking, or outdoor spaces.

Analyze the pricing of these comparable listings across different timeframes, including weekdays, weekends, and peak seasons such as holidays or special events. Pay attention to how prices fluctuate during high-demand periods and slow seasons. Additionally, note any discounts offered for longer stays, such as weekly or monthly rates.

Evaluate the reviews of competing properties to understand what guests value most and whether any gaps in service or amenities could be opportunities for you to stand out. If your property offers unique features, such as exceptional decor, luxury upgrades, or pet-friendly options, factor these into your pricing to justify a higher rate.

Leverage pricing tools or dynamic pricing software, which can analyze local market trends and adjust your rates automatically to remain competitive. Regularly review and update your pricing strategy to align with market changes, ensuring you maximize occupancy and profitability while providing value to your guests.

Consider Your Costs

When determining the pricing for your short-term rental, it's essential to take a comprehensive approach by factoring in all associated costs to ensure your rate is both competitive and profitable. Begin by calculating your fixed costs, such as your mortgage or rent payments, property taxes, homeowner's insurance, and any HOA or condominium fees. Next, account for variable monthly expenses, including utilities like electricity, water, gas, internet, and cable.

Don't forget to include hosting-specific costs. These can include cleaning fees, whether you hire a professional cleaning service or purchase cleaning supplies for self-maintenance. Factor in the cost of consumable items you provide for guests, such as toiletries, coffee, tea, paper towels, and replacement linens. These should also be included if you use a property management service, dynamic pricing software, or listing platforms that charge service fees or commissions.

Additionally, set aside a budget for ongoing maintenance and unexpected repairs, as wear and tear is inevitable with frequent guests. Consider including a portion for marketing expenses, such as professional photography or promoted listings, to attract more bookings.

Once you've tallied all costs, establish a pricing structure that covers these expenses and generates a reasonable profit margin. Regularly review and update your pricing strategy to align with changes in your costs, market demand, and local competition, ensuring your rental remains financially sustainable and successful.

Use Airbnb's Price Tips

Airbnb offers a feature called "Price Tips" that can help you set the right price for your listing. Price Tips uses data like your location, listing details, and historical booking data to recommend a price range for your listing. While you don't have to follow these recommendations, they can be a helpful starting point.

Adjust Your Price Based on Demand

Adjusting your rental price based on market demand is a key strategy to maximize your occupancy and profitability. Monitor your booking trends regularly to identify patterns and adjust your pricing accordingly. If you're receiving a high volume of inquiries and bookings, especially during peak seasons, holidays, or special local events, this may signal strong demand, and you can raise your price slightly to reflect this increased interest. Be mindful to avoid pricing too high, as this may deter potential guests, but moderate increases can help you capitalize on high demand while maintaining competitive pricing.

On the other hand, if your property isn't generating enough interest or bookings, consider lowering your price to make your listing more attractive to potential guests. Lowering your price can also help fill gaps in your calendar during off-peak seasons or last-minute bookings. Additionally, offering special discounts or promotions, such as a limited-time offer or a deal for longer stays, can encourage guests to book when demand is low.

To find the optimal price point, utilize dynamic pricing tools or software that analyze local market trends and adjust your rates in real-time. Regularly assess your pricing strategy based on factors like the time of year, local events, competitor pricing, and your property's performance. By being flexible and responsive to demand, you can strike the right balance between attracting bookings and maximizing revenue.

Be Flexible

Remember that pricing for your short-term rental is not fixed and should be adjusted regularly to reflect changes in demand, seasonality, and other market factors. As market conditions fluctuate, such as during peak travel seasons, local events, or shifts in guest behavior, it's important to remain flexible and open to modifying your pricing to stay competitive and optimize occupancy. For example, you may choose to increase rates during high-demand periods like holidays or special events, or offer discounts during off-peak months to attract more bookings.

Experimenting with different pricing strategies can also help you determine what works best for your property. You might test out varying nightly rates, offering weekly or monthly discounts, or introducing promotional rates to encourage longer stays or last-minute bookings. Additionally, consider implementing dynamic pricing tools or software that automatically adjusts rates based on local trends, competitor pricing, and booking patterns.

Regularly review your pricing strategy to ensure it aligns with your goals, whether that's maximizing occupancy, increasing revenue, or attracting repeat guests. Be proactive in monitoring your performance and be willing to make changes if you're not hitting your targets. By staying adaptable and willing to experiment, you can find the optimal pricing strategy that works for both you and your guests.

Pricing is just one part of the hosting experience, so make sure you're also providing a great guest experience to keep your guests coming back. In the next chapter, we'll cover how to attract more guests by describing a winning listing.

***

Need more help pricing your rental listing? Get the Rental Space Pricing Workbook on Etsy *with comparison, amenity, and budgeting worksheets to help you perfectly price your rental.*

Chapter 5 Writing a Winning Listing Description: How to Attract Guests with YourWords

Your short-term rental listing description is your chance to sell your space to potential guests. It's important to make sure your description is clear, accurate, and engaging to attract the right guests. Here are some tips for writing a winning listing description:

Be Specific

When crafting the description for your short-term vacation rental listing, it's essential to emphasize what makes your space truly unique and set it apart from the competition. Start by highlighting any special features or amenities that will appeal to potential guests. For example, if your property includes a private pool, jacuzzi, or hot tub, be sure to mention these luxurious extras and how they contribute to a relaxing stay. If your rental has a balcony, terrace, or patio with a scenic view—whether it's of the ocean, mountains, or city skyline—describe how guests can enjoy the view, whether it's for morning coffee, sunset cocktails, or stargazing at night.

Consider other distinctive elements of your space, such as high-end appliances, smart home technology, or a cozy fireplace that creates a warm ambiance. If your rental is pet-friendly, provide details about your pet policies and any special amenities like a dog bed or fenced yard. If your home is within walking distance of local attractions, the beach, or popular restaurants, mention the convenience of the location.

Incorporate details about the atmosphere and décor, such as a thoughtfully designed interior with stylish furnishings or locally inspired art. Guests appreciate knowing what kind of experience they can expect, so be sure to describe the ambiance of the space—whether it's perfect for a romantic getaway, a family retreat, or an adventurous stay.

By clearly outlining the unique features and benefits of your property, you'll create a compelling listing that gives potential guests a vivid picture of what to expect, helping them feel more confident about booking and ensuring your property stands out in a crowded market.

Use Descriptive Language

When writing your short-term vacation rental listing, it's crucial to use descriptive and engaging language that allows potential guests to truly visualize your space. Rather than using vague terms like "nice" to describe your living room or other areas, take the time to provide vivid, detailed descriptions that highlight the room's unique features. For instance, instead of saying, "We have a nice living room," try saying something like, "Our bright and airy living room boasts large windows that flood the space with natural light, creating a warm and inviting atmosphere. The room is furnished with a plush sectional sofa and two armchairs, offering comfortable seating for up to six guests, perfect for relaxing or enjoying a movie night on the 55-inch flat-screen TV."

Incorporate sensory details to make the space feel tangible, such as the texture of the furniture, the colors of the décor, and how guests might feel while in the room. You can also highlight the purpose of the space, like whether it's ideal for unwinding with a book, hosting a family game night, or enjoying conversation with friends. Mention any thoughtful touches, like soft throw blankets or decorative pillows, that create an inviting atmosphere. By painting a clear and enticing picture of your space, you help guests imagine themselves there, which can increase their confidence in booking your property.

Highlight Your Location

Your location is one of the most important selling points for your short-term vacation rental, so be sure to highlight the unique attractions and amenities that make your area special. Provide detailed information about nearby points of interest, such as local parks, museums, galleries, or historical sites, that guests can explore during their stay. If your property is close to popular outdoor activities like hiking trails, biking routes, or water sports, make sure to mention these options for adventure seekers.

If your rental is located near vibrant dining options, talk about the best restaurants, cafes, or food markets within walking distance or a short drive away. Highlight any renowned local dishes or must-try eateries that guests shouldn't miss. Similarly, if your property is near entertainment venues such as theaters, concert halls, or sporting events, let potential guests know about these opportunities to experience local culture and nightlife.

For families, mention any family-friendly attractions like zoos, aquariums, or amusement parks. For those looking for relaxation, point out nearby spas, scenic spots for picnics, or tranquil nature walks. If your property is conveniently located to public transportation or has easy access to major highways, be sure to mention this to add value for guests who may not have their own vehicle.

By providing detailed information about the surrounding area, you give guests a clear sense of what they can expect and inspire them to explore, making your rental an even more appealing option.

Provide Accurate Information

It's essential to ensure that all the information in your listing description is accurate and up-to-date. This includes providing precise details about the number of bedrooms, the layout and square footage of the space, and the amenities that are included. For example, clearly specify how many beds are in each bedroom, what types of mattresses are provided (e.g., queen, king, twin), and if there are additional sleeping arrangements like a sofa bed or pull-out couch.

In addition to the basics, accurately describe the layout of the property—whether it has an open-plan living area, multiple floors, or specific areas such as a private office, home gym, or a designated workspace. This helps guests better understand how the space will accommodate their needs. Be transparent about the amenities offered, such as Wi-Fi, air conditioning, heating, kitchen appliances, and laundry facilities. If you provide any additional perks like a hot tub, pool, or barbecue grill, make sure these are highlighted.

Avoid using vague terms or exaggerations that could lead to misunderstandings. For instance, don't simply say "large kitchen" without clarifying whether it's fully equipped for cooking meals, has modern appliances, or offers any special features like a breakfast nook or island seating. Providing accurate, clear, and thorough information not only sets proper expectations but also helps build trust with your guests. This reduces the likelihood of miscommunication and negative reviews, ensuring a smooth and pleasant experience for both you and your guests.

Use Keywords

Incorporating relevant keywords into your listing description is a key strategy to improve your visibility and increase your chances of appearing higher in short-term rental search results. Think about the specific terms potential guests might use when searching for a property like yours, and strategically integrate those keywords throughout your description. This will not only enhance your listing's searchability but also make it more likely that guests will find your property when they are browsing for specific features.

For example, if your space is pet-friendly, make sure to prominently include the term "pet-friendly" in your description, as this is a popular search term for travelers who want to bring their pets along. Similarly, if your property is located near a popular attraction or landmark, such as a beach, national park, or downtown area, be sure to include those keywords, such as "close to the beach" or "walking distance to downtown," so that your listing appears when guests search for proximity to those areas.

Other useful keywords might include "family-friendly," "luxury," "hot tub," "pool," "private patio," or "business travel," depending on the unique features and target audience of your property. Be careful not to overstuff your description with too many keywords, as this can come across as unnatural or forced. Instead, aim to seamlessly incorporate these terms while still providing a detailed, compelling narrative of what your property offers. Using the right keywords effectively will help attract more guests and improve your chances of a higher ranking in search results.

Your listing description is just one part of the hosting experience, so make sure you're also providing a great guest experience to keep your guests coming back. In the next chapter, we'll cover how to communicate with guests and provide a great check-in experience.

Chapter 6 Guest Communication: How to Interact with Your Guests Before and During Their Stay

Clear and timely communication is key to providing a great guest experience. Here are some tips for communicating with your guests before and during their stay:

Respond Quickly

Responding promptly to potential guests' inquiries is crucial for building a positive reputation and establishing trust. When a guest reaches out with a question or inquiry, make it a priority to respond as quickly as possible, ideally within a few hours or by the end of the day. A fast response shows that you are attentive, reliable, and committed to providing excellent customer service, which can make a significant difference in whether a guest chooses to book your property.

If you are unable to respond immediately, try to acknowledge their message as soon as possible, letting them know that you've received it and will get back to them shortly. This reassures the guest that their inquiry is being taken seriously. If you can, aim to respond within 24 hours or less, as quick replies help you stand out in a competitive market where guests may be considering multiple options.

Providing clear, friendly, and detailed responses will also demonstrate your professionalism and make potential guests feel more comfortable with their decision to book with you. A timely and helpful reply can increase your chances of securing a booking and earning positive reviews, which in turn can boost the visibility and success of your listing.

Be Clear and Detailed

When communicating with guests, it's essential to be as clear, thorough, and helpful as possible in your responses. Take the time to answer each of their questions in full, providing all the details they need to make an informed decision. If they ask about amenities, be specific about what is available and how to use it. For example, if they inquire about the Wi-Fi, provide the network name and password, and mention any specific instructions for connecting. If they ask about local attractions, include suggestions with relevant details such as distance from your property, hours of operation, and any special events happening in the area during their stay.

Additionally, anticipate any other questions or concerns they might have, even if they haven't asked yet. For example, if you know that parking can be tricky in your neighborhood, proactively share information about where guests can park or offer alternatives. Being proactive about sharing this kind of helpful information will set the right expectations for their stay, reduce any potential confusion, and foster a sense of trust.

Clear communication is key in preventing misunderstandings, as it helps guests know exactly what to expect. Whether it's about the check-in process, house rules, or special accommodations, the more detailed and transparent you are, the more confident guests will feel about their decision to book with you. This can lead to a smoother guest experience, fewer issues during their stay, and ultimately, positive reviews.

Use The Listing Platform's Messaging System

All communication between hosts and guests should take place through the short-term rental platform's messaging system. This method ensures that there is a clear, verifiable record of all interactions, which can be invaluable if any disputes or issues arise during or after the guest's stay. Having a written record allows both parties to refer back to prior conversations for clarification, which helps to resolve misunderstandings more effectively.

Uusing a platform's messaging system ensures that both hosts and guests are protected by the short-term rental platform's policies and guidelines. These policies often include protections regarding cancellations, refunds, disputes, and behavior expectations, which can offer peace of mind for both parties. By keeping communication within the platform, you also reduce the risk of sensitive personal information being shared outside of secure channels, further safeguarding both the host and guest's privacy.

In the event of a problem, having all communication logged through the platform allows the rental service to step in and mediate, if necessary, offering both the host and guest an impartial third-party resource for resolving the situation. By adhering to the platform's communication protocols, you help create a safe and transparent experience for all parties involved.

Provide Check-In Information

Before your guests arrive, it's crucial to provide them with clear, detailed check-in instructions to ensure a seamless arrival experience. Start by offering step-by-step guidance on how to access your space, including the address and specific directions, especially if your property is in a complex or hard-to-find location. If there are any special instructions for locating the entrance or navigating the property, such as the need to enter through a particular door or gate, be sure to mention these clearly.

If your property uses a keypad or lockbox for entry, provide guests with the necessary access codes or combination well in advance. It's also helpful to remind them of any important security instructions, like where to find the key or how to operate the lock system. If you're meeting guests in person, specify the exact time and place for key handoff or check-in.

Additionally, provide any other relevant details that could make their arrival more convenient, such as where to park, how to access amenities (like elevators or common areas), and any other information that might prevent confusion, like a list of items to bring (towels, pool pass, etc.). If you have a manual or house guide with important information about the property, make sure they know where to find it.

By offering clear, well-structured check-in information ahead of time, you help set the right expectations for your guests and reduce the chance of delays or miscommunications. This ensures a smooth check-in process, allowing your guests to feel welcomed and settled in right from the start.

Check-In with Guests

During your guest's stay, it's important to check in with them periodically to ensure everything is going smoothly and to address any needs or concerns they may have. You can do this through the short-term rental platform's messaging system, sending a friendly and personalized message to ask how their stay is going and if they need anything. If you're located nearby, offering to stop by in person to check in and provide assistance can create an even more welcoming atmosphere.

Your check-in message should be thoughtful and proactive, asking specific questions that show you're genuinely concerned about their experience. For example, you might ask if they are comfortable, if everything in the home is functioning as expected, or if they need recommendations for local activities or restaurants. This kind of communication lets guests know that you're available to help, should any issues arise, and that you care about their comfort and satisfaction.

Additionally, by staying in touch during their stay, you show that you're an engaged and responsible host, which can help build trust and create a positive relationship. Timely check-ins can also give guests an opportunity to mention any issues they may not have brought up initially, allowing you to address them before they escalate. Overall, being attentive and responsive during your guest's stay helps ensure they have a smooth and enjoyable experience, which can lead to better reviews and repeat bookings.

Be Professional and Courteous

When communicating with guests, it's essential to maintain a high level of professionalism and courtesy at all times. This means using polite and respectful language in all your interactions, ensuring your tone is friendly and accommodating. It's important to be mindful of their privacy and avoid over-communicating unless necessary, respecting their space while still being available for assistance when needed.

Always be prompt in addressing any issues or concerns guests may raise, responding to their inquiries as quickly as possible, ideally within a few hours or by the end of the day. If a guest encounters a problem during their stay, acknowledge their concern with empathy, express understanding, and take swift action to resolve the issue. Clear, considerate communication will help foster trust and demonstrate your commitment to providing a positive guest experience.

Ensure that your communication style remains consistent and professional throughout their entire stay, whether it's handling booking details, check-in instructions, or any follow-up after their departure. By treating guests with respect and professionalism, you create a welcoming environment that not only resolves issues efficiently but also encourages positive reviews and repeat bookings.

Chapter 7 Managing Bookings: How to Handle Reservations and Cancellations

Managing bookings is a critical part of hosting on short-term rental. Here are some tips for handling reservations and cancellations:

Accepting or Declining Booking Requests

When a guest submits a booking request on platforms like Airbnb, you have 24 hours to review and either accept or decline it. To make an informed decision, take the time to carefully review the guest's profile, paying attention to their ratings, reviews, and any feedback from previous hosts. This will give you valuable insight into their past behavior, communication style, and whether they align with your expectations for a respectful and responsible guest. Look for signs of guests who are thoughtful, respectful of property, and have a history of positive reviews, as this can help ensure a smooth experience for both parties.

If you decide to decline the booking request, it's important to provide the guest with a clear and polite explanation for your decision. Offering a reason, such as schedule conflicts, property limitations, or any other valid concern, helps maintain transparency and ensures the guest understands the rationale behind your choice. Providing this feedback also fosters a positive relationship, as it shows that you are respectful and considerate of their time and efforts in reaching out.

While declining a booking request is a part of the hosting process, taking the time to thoughtfully assess each guest and communicate clearly helps to maintain a positive reputation and encourages mutual respect between hosts and guests.

Setting Reservation Requirements

As a host, you have the ability to set specific reservation requirements for your listing, such as a minimum stay, maximum number of guests, or any other conditions that align with your preferences and property limitations. For example, you may require a minimum number of nights for a booking, especially during peak seasons, or set a maximum guest limit to ensure your space accommodates your guests comfortably. You may also consider additional requirements, such as age restrictions or specific check-in/check-out times.

To avoid any confusion or misunderstandings, it's crucial to clearly communicate these reservation requirements in your listing description. Be explicit about these conditions right from the start, detailing things like the minimum or maximum length of stay, the maximum number of guests your property can comfortably accommodate, and any other important terms. For instance, if you require a longer stay during busy weekends or holidays, mention the specific dates or periods when this applies.

By making your reservation requirements clear in the listing, you help set proper expectations for potential guests and prevent any surprises later on. It's also helpful to reiterate these terms during the booking process and confirm them in your communication with guests before finalizing their reservation. This approach not only helps ensure a smooth booking experience but also improves guest satisfaction by providing transparency and clarity.

Handling Cancellations

If a guest decides to cancel their reservation, you have the option to issue a refund based on the terms outlined in your cancellation policy. It's essential that your cancellation policy is clear, transparent, and easily accessible to potential guests. Be sure to include a detailed explanation of the policy in your listing description, covering key points such as the notice period required for a full or partial refund, any non-refundable fees, and the specific time frames that determine the refund amount. This will help set clear expectations and reduce the likelihood of misunderstandings. Additionally, it's important to consistently adhere to your cancellation policy, ensuring that any cancellations are handled according to the guidelines you've established.

If, for any reason, you need to cancel a reservation, it's crucial to notify the guest as soon as possible. Provide them with a prompt and clear explanation for the cancellation, whether it's due to unforeseen maintenance issues, personal emergencies, or other circumstances. Offering an honest and empathetic reason will help maintain trust with your guests. Whenever possible, provide them with alternative solutions, such as rebooking their stay on different dates, recommending similar properties, or offering assistance with finding nearby accommodations. Open and respectful communication during this process can help preserve your reputation as a reliable host and minimize any negative impact on the guest's experience.

Updating Your Calendar

It's essential to keep your calendar consistently up-to-date to prevent any risk of double bookings, which can lead to confusion and dissatisfaction for both you and your guests. Regularly review and update your availability to ensure that your listing accurately reflects the dates your space is free for booking. If your property is unavailable for any reason—such as maintenance, personal use, or travel—be sure to block those dates off on your calendar as soon as possible.

Additionally, if your booking platform allows, consider syncing your calendar with other platforms where your property is listed to avoid discrepancies between them. This helps streamline the process and ensures that availability is consistent across all booking channels. For example, if you use Airbnb, Booking.com, and Vrbo, syncing calendars between these platforms ensures that when a booking is made on one site, the dates automatically get blocked on others.

By proactively blocking unavailable dates and keeping your calendar accurate, you'll prevent guests from attempting to book dates that aren't available, minimizing the chance for booking conflicts and maintaining a smooth guest experience. Furthermore, ensuring that your calendar is updated in real-time helps build trust with potential guests, showing them that you are an attentive and reliable host.

Handling Last-Minute Reservations

When you receive a last-minute reservation request, it's important to take the time to carefully review the guest's profile and ratings before accepting the booking. Look for any feedback from previous hosts to gauge the guest's reliability and whether they are likely to follow your house rules and respect your property. Pay attention to any red flags, such as poor communication or issues with past stays, which could indicate potential problems.

In addition to reviewing their profile, it's a good idea to confirm the details of the reservation directly with the guest. Reach out to them through the messaging system to clarify any necessary information, such as their expected check-in time, the number of guests, or any special requests they may have.

This not only ensures that all the details align with your expectations, but also allows you to establish communication with the guest, helping to set the tone for a smooth and pleasant stay.

By thoroughly vetting last-minute reservation requests, you minimize the risk of surprises and ensure that the booking aligns with your availability and house rules. Clear communication with the guest helps ensure that both you and the guest are on the same page, creating a positive experience for both parties and reducing the likelihood of any issues during their stay.

Handling No-Shows

If a guest fails to show up for their reservation, you may still be entitled to payment based on the terms outlined in your cancellation policy. It's crucial to refer to your specific policy to determine whether a no-show qualifies for a full or partial payment, depending on how far in advance the guest canceled (if at all) and your established guidelines for last- minute cancellations or no-shows.

To protect yourself and maintain a clear record, be sure to document all communication with the guest related to the no-show. This includes any messages or calls about their late arrival, cancellation, or failure to show up. Keep a detailed log of when the reservation was made, any discussions or issues that arose prior to the guest's check-in date, and any actions you took to try to contact them.

Additionally, follow the specific procedures set by the short-term vacation rental platform you use for reporting a no-show. Many platforms provide clear steps for reporting no-shows and handling cancellations, including how to document the situation and any evidence of the guest's failure to attend. Adhering to these steps will ensure that you remain compliant with platform policies and may help you recoup any losses associated with the missed booking. Taking these actions also reinforces your professionalism and helps protect your business in the event of future disputes.

Chapter 8 Preparing for Check-In: What to Do Before Your Guests Arrive

Preparing for check-in is an important part of hosting on short-term rental. Here are some tips for what to do before your guests arrive:

Clean and Tidy Your Space

Before your guests arrive, it's essential to ensure that your space is spotless, well-organized, and ready for their stay. This includes performing a thorough cleaning of all areas of the property. Start by vacuuming and dusting all floors, furniture, and surfaces, ensuring that corners and hidden areas are also addressed. Wipe down and sanitize all frequently touched surfaces, such as countertops, light switches, doorknobs, and remote controls, to maintain a hygienic environment.

The bathroom and kitchen require special attention. Clean and sanitize all bathroom fixtures, including the sink, shower or bathtub, toilet, and mirrors. Replace used or dirty towels with fresh, clean ones, and ensure that toiletries like soap, shampoo, and toilet paper are fully stocked. In the kitchen, clean all appliances (fridge, microwave, stove, and oven), countertops, and sinks. Check that dishes, cutlery, and cookware are thoroughly cleaned and put away.

Ensure that fresh, high-quality linens are provided for each guest, including bed sheets, pillowcases, and towels, to make them feel comfortable during their stay. If your rental offers additional amenities like blankets or throws, these should be neatly arranged and cleaned as well.

If you have decided to hire a cleaning service to manage your rental space turnover, it is crucial to communicate your expectations and schedule well in advance. Ideally, notify the cleaning service at least 48-72 hours prior to your guest's check-in to allow enough time for the cleaning team to properly prepare the space. This ensures that the space is thoroughly cleaned and ready for the next guest without any last-minute rush. Regular communication with your cleaning service helps maintain consistency and ensures that every guest enjoys a pristine, welcoming environment upon arrival.

Stock Up on Supplies

To ensure that your guests have a comfortable and hassle- free stay, it's important to stock up on a variety of essential supplies that they may need throughout their visit.

Begin by ensuring that the bathroom is well-stocked with high-quality toilet paper, hand soap, body wash, shampoo, conditioner, and clean towels. Consider providing a few extra rolls of toilet paper and additional soap or shampoo, as some guests may appreciate the convenience of having extra on hand during longer stays.

In the kitchen, make sure to provide all the basic supplies necessary for guests to prepare meals and enjoy their time in the space. This includes a complete set of dishes, glasses, mugs, and utensils (such as knives, forks, spoons, and steak knives). Ensure there are enough pots, pans, and cooking utensils like spatulas, ladles, and a cutting board for meal prep. If you provide baking sheets, mixing bowls, or a coffee maker, ensure they are clean, functional, and ready for use.

It's also a good idea to stock essential pantry items like salt, pepper, oil, and basic spices for guests who want to cook, as well as coffee, tea, and sugar for those who may need a caffeine boost. Depending on the type of guests you cater to, you might also want to consider providing other amenities such as a toaster, microwave, blender, or rice cooker.

Having these supplies readily available helps enhance the overall guest experience, reducing the chances of complaints and ensuring your space is well-equipped for any kind of stay. Replenishing supplies regularly between bookings ensures that you maintain a consistent standard and your guests always feel comfortable and cared for.

Test Appliances and Electronics

Before your guests arrive, it's essential to thoroughly test all appliances and electronics in your space to ensure everything is functioning properly. This includes checking major appliances like the oven, refrigerator, and microwave to ensure they're working as expected. Make sure the oven heats evenly, the refrigerator is maintaining a proper temperature, and the microwave is fully operational for your guests' convenience.

In addition to the kitchen appliances, pay attention to any other electronics provided in the space, such as the television, sound systems, or any smart home devices. Verify that the TV is connected to the correct channels or streaming services and that it has the necessary remotes available and functioning. Test any entertainment devices or game consoles if you have them in your space, ensuring they are set up and ready for use.

Wi-Fi is another critical element of guest satisfaction, so double-check that your internet connection is strong and reliable. Ensure that the Wi-Fi password is correct and easily accessible for your guests. If you provide any additional technology, like Bluetooth speakers, smart thermostats, or home security systems, test these as well to make sure they are functional and easy for guests to operate.

If any appliance or piece of technology isn't working properly, take the necessary steps to repair or replace it before your guests arrive. This will help avoid any disruptions during their stay and prevent any frustration or negative reviews. It's always better to address these issues proactively to ensure your guests have a seamless and enjoyable experience.

Provide a Welcome Guide

Provide your guests with a comprehensive and easy-to-read welcome guide that will enhance their experience during their stay. This guide should include key details about your space, such as the Wi-Fi password, instructions for using appliances and electronics, and any specific rules or guidelines they need to follow. For example, explain how to operate the thermostat, how to use the washing machine, and any safety procedures they should be aware of, such as emergency exits or how to contact you in case of an issue.

In addition to the practical information, include a section dedicated to recommendations for local attractions, restaurants, cafes, shops, and entertainment options. Highlight nearby parks, museums, landmarks, or hiking trails that guests might enjoy. You can also provide personal insights into your favorite places, such as hidden gems or local hotspots that might not be well-known to tourists. Including a map of the area or links to local resources will also help guests explore with ease.

Make sure your guide is visually appealing and easy to navigate, with clearly labeled sections and organized content. Guests will appreciate having this information readily available, making them feel more comfortable and informed during their stay. A well-thought-out welcome guide can also reduce questions and help avoid any confusion, providing your guests with a smooth and enjoyable experience.

For your convenience, you can find a customizable, user-friendly Short-Term Vacation Rental Welcome Guide template, along with other helpful cleaning, maintenance and supply checklists, tools and other resources for rental owners and hospitality professionals, in my Etsy shop – Otis Design Boutique. This will save you time and ensure your welcome guide is both professional and tailored to your specific rental property.

Leave a Personal Touch

Add a personal touch to your space to make your guests feel truly welcomed and appreciated. Simple gestures can make a big difference in creating a memorable experience. Consider leaving a thoughtful welcome note expressing your excitement about hosting them and offering any helpful information they may need during their stay. A small gift can also go a long way — whether it's a local handmade item, a small plant, or something that reflects the area's culture.

To enhance their comfort, you could leave a selection of snacks or beverages for your guests to enjoy upon arrival. Think about including locally sourced treats or a bottle of wine, craft beer, or bottled water to make them feel at home. These little comforts can be especially appreciated after a long journey.

One of my favorite ways to go above and beyond is by preparing a welcome basket. This basket can be filled with a mix ofthoughtful items that guests might appreciate during their stay. For example, local snacks or artisanal products from nearby farmers' markets, sunscreen, hand sanitizer, and even personal care items like lip balm or travel-sized toiletries— things guests may forget to pack. Including a few branded items, such as a custom keychain, reusable water bottle, or tote bag with your rental logo, gives guests a practical souvenir to remember their stay.

By leaving a personal touch like this, you help create a welcoming environment where guests feel valued and cared for, which can encourage positive reviews and repeat bookings.

Confirm Check-In Details

It's important to confirm all check-in details with your guests well in advance of their arrival to ensure a smooth and stress-free experience. Start by confirming the date and time of their arrival, allowing you to anticipate when they'll need access to your space. Ask if they plan to arrive during specific hours (e.g., early evening or late night) so you can make any necessary adjustments.

Provide clear, step-by-step instructions on how to access your property. If you're using a keyless entry system, share the code along with the procedure for entering, ensuring that they understand how to use it properly. If you plan to meet them in person, provide your contact information, including a phone number where you can be reached if needed, and arrange a specific time to greet them.

In addition, be sure to include any necessary information about parking or special access points, such as gate codes, lockbox locations, or building entrances. If your property is in a complex or hard-to-find area, you might want to include landmarks or specific directions to help guests avoid getting lost.

Finally, include any other relevant details, like Wi-Fi information, appliance instructions, or specific rules for check-in. This thorough communication ensures that your guests will feel confident upon arrival and can start enjoying their stay without confusion or frustration.

These tips ensure that your guests have a comfortable and enjoyable stay from the moment they arrive. In the next chapter, we'll cover how to welcome your guests and provide an excellent check-in experience.

Chapter 9 Welcoming Your Guests: How to Provide a Great Check-In Experience

Providing a great check-in experience is crucial to setting the tone for your guests' stay. Although meeting guests is not required, going above and beyond to provide the best experience can go a long way when it comes to reviews.

Here are some tips for welcoming your guests and making sure they feel comfortable:

Be on Time

If you are planning to meet your guests for check-in, it's essential to arrive on time to create a positive first impression and demonstrate to your guests that you value their time and are committed to providing them with a seamless experience. Timeliness sets the tone for their entire stay, showing that you are organized, reliable, and professional.

If for any reason you anticipate being late, it's important to proactively communicate with your guests as soon as possible. Let them know the revised check-in time and apologize for any inconvenience. Offer an estimated arrival time, and provide alternative solutions if necessary, such as instructions for self-check-in or a contingency plan if they need to wait briefly.

Always stay in close contact with your guests, keeping them updated about your arrival status. This transparency ensures that guests feel well taken care of and reassured, ultimately contributing to a positive guest experience from the moment they arrive.

Greet Your Guests

When your guests arrive, greet them with a friendly smile and a warm, welcoming demeanor. Take a moment to introduce yourself and express how excited you are to have them stay in your space. Ask if they have any questions or concerns about their stay, such as how to operate appliances or where to find amenities. This open and approachable communication helps to create an inviting atmosphere, making your guests feel comfortable and cared for right from the start.

Show Them Around

When your guests arrive, take the time to give them a thorough tour of your space to ensure they feel completely comfortable and well-informed. Start by showing them the key areas of the home, including where to find extra towels, linens, and blankets, and explain how to access the Wi-Fi, including the password and any troubleshooting tips if necessary.

Walk them through how to use any appliances, such as the oven, dishwasher, microwave, and any other key items they might need during their stay. If you have a smart TV, sound system, or other technology, provide clear instructions on how to operate these devices.

It's also important to point out any safety features in your space. Make sure your guests know the locations of emergency exits, fire extinguishers, first aid kits, and any security systems, such as cameras or alarms, that are in place for their safety. If there are any specific house rules related to safety or security, explain those as well.

Highlighting these details not only helps your guests feel more at ease but also shows that you're dedicated to their comfort and safety during their stay. It can also reduce the chances of them needing to reach out for assistance later on, making their experience smoother and more enjoyable.

Provide Local Recommendations

Providing your guests with personalized local recommendations is a great way to enhance their stay and show that you're familiar with the area. Take the time to curate a list of your favorite restaurants, cafes, and dining spots, highlighting different types of cuisine or unique local experiences. Include details like whether reservations are recommended or if there are any must-try dishes at a particular restaurant.

For entertainment and exploration, recommend nearby attractions, such as parks, museums, hiking trails, or scenic viewpoints, based on their interests. If your area is known for outdoor activities, suggest places for cycling, kayaking, or fishing. Be sure to include any seasonal events or festivals happening during their visit that they might want to check out.

If your guests are looking to shop, share insights on local boutiques, markets, and unique shops that offer one-of-a-kind items or locally made products. Highlight any hidden gems that might not be found in typical tourist guides.

To make their experience even more seamless, provide a map of the area with key locations marked, such as recommended spots, local landmarks, or even your favorite spots for a relaxing stroll.

Offering clear directions to these places, along with any relevant tips like parking or transportation options, can help guests make the most of their time. Providing such information not only helps guests navigate the area with ease but also demonstrates your commitment to offering an exceptional and memorable stay.

Answer Any Questions

It's essential to address any questions your guests may have promptly and thoroughly, ensuring they feel well-informed and confident throughout their stay. This includes questions about your space, such as how to operate appliances, how to use amenities, or any special instructions related to your property. Make sure to clarify important details like check-out procedures, the location of key items such as extra towels or trash bins, and any house rules they need to follow.

Guests may also have questions about parking arrangements, so be prepared to explain parking options clearly, including designated spaces, street parking availability, or any special instructions for parking permits. If local transportation is a consideration for your guests, provide information on nearby bus or train stations, taxi services, or ride-sharing options like Uber or Lyft. You might also want to inform them of any special routes, public transport passes, or tips for getting around town conveniently.

If a guest asks a question you're unsure about, don't hesitate to offer to look up the information or direct them to someone who can help. Being transparent and resourceful will not only build trust but also reinforce your dedication to providing an excellent guest experience. Taking the extra step to offer guidance, whether it's about your space or the surrounding area, will make your guests feel supported and cared for during their stay.

Leave Contact Information

It's important to ensure your guests have easy access to your contact information in case they need assistance or have any concerns during their stay. Make sure to provide your phone number, email address, or other preferred methods of communication clearly at the beginning of their stay, either in your welcome guide or upon check-in. This gives them a direct line to you should they encounter any issues or have questions about the property, amenities, or the local area.

Additionally, establish clear expectations for your response time, and make sure to be as responsive as possible when your guests reach out. Whether it's via text, phone call, or email, aim to respond promptly—ideally within an hour or less. This will reassure your guests that they can count on you for timely assistance, fostering trust and making them feel valued throughout their stay.

If you're unavailable or out of reach for any reason, consider providing an alternative contact person, like a property manager or a trusted friend, who can handle urgent issues in your absence.

This ensures your guests never feel left without support, even if you are temporarily unavailable. Clear communication, quick responses, and accessibility will contribute to a positive guest experience and help avoid any frustrations or misunderstandings.

Chapter 10 House Rules: Setting Expectations for Your Guests

Establishing clear house rules is an essential part of hosting on short-term rental. These rules help ensure that your guests understand what is expected of them during their stay and can help prevent any issues from arising.

Here are some tips for setting house rules for your short-term rental listing:

Keep It Simple

When creating your house rules, it's crucial to keep them clear, concise, and easy to follow. Avoid overwhelming your guests with an extensive list of rules or overly complex instructions. Focus on the essential guidelines that will ensure the safety, comfort, and enjoyment of everyone during their stay. Consider including rules that pertain to basic things like noise levels, smoking, pet policies, and the number of guests allowed, as these are key to maintaining a positive atmosphere and protecting your space.

To make things even easier for guests, organize your house rules in a simple, bullet-point format and highlight any non-negotiable rules that directly impact the safety or upkeep of the property. For example, rules about locking doors when leaving the property, disposing of trash, or respecting quiet hours could be listed as key points. This not only ensures guests can quickly reference them but also helps establish expectations upfront, which can prevent misunderstandings later.

While it's important to have rules, avoid making them overly restrictive or burdensome. The goal is to create an environment where guests feel welcome, comfortable, and informed, not restricted. If there are any specific instructions regarding appliances, the use of common areas, or check-out procedures, make sure they're written in a friendly, approachable tone. By keeping your house rules simple yet clear, you'll help foster a pleasant and respectful guest experience.

Be Specific

To maintain a welcoming and safe environment for all guests, it's important to be very specific about what is and is not allowed within your space. Clearly outline any restrictions such as no smoking, no pets, or no parties, and make sure these rules are easy to find in your listing and in your house rules. For instance, if smoking is prohibited, state it clearly and explain that smoking indoors will incur a cleaning fee to remove any lingering odors and maintain the space for future guests. Similarly, if pets are not allowed, be specific about the type of animals you do not permit, and explain that any violations will result in additional charges or even a request for the guest to leave.

Make sure your guests understand the consequences of violating these rules. For example, if a party is thrown in your space, outline the potential penalties, which could include a cleaning fee, an additional charge for damages, or even eviction from the property without a refund. By setting clear expectations up front, you can prevent misunderstandings and avoid situations where guests feel blindsided by rules they didn't know about.

In your listing and house rules, communicate these policies in a respectful yet firm manner. While it's important to protect your property, it's equally important to ensure that guests feel comfortable and aware of your expectations. You could also offer a friendly reminder about these policies upon check-in to ensure guests have a final opportunity to ask questions or clarify anything before their stay begins.

Communicate Clearly

It's essential to ensure that your house rules are clearly commu- nicated to your guests from the moment they book until they check out. To start, include the rules in your listing description so potential guests can review them before booking. This transparency sets clear expectations right away and can help avoid any misunderstandings later.

In addition to listing them upfront, send a friendly reminder of the rules in a message to your guests before their arrival. This message can be sent a few days before check-in, giving them time to review and ask questions. Make sure the rules are easily accessible, and consider tailoring the message to reflect any specific house rules that may apply to the individual reservation (e.g., quiet hours, pet policy, or parking instructions).

For further clarity, you could also create a printed or laminated card with the house rules and place it in a highly visible location within your space. A great spot could be near the entryway or on the kitchen counter, where guests will see it immediately upon arrival. The card should be easy to read, with bullet points or numbered lists for quick reference. You could even add a friendly note like, "Please let us know if you have any questions about these rules—your comfort and safety are important to us."

By communicating your house rules clearly and in multiple ways, you help ensure that your guests are informed and prepared for a smooth, enjoyable stay.

Be Flexible

Setting clear expectations for your guests is a key part of ensuring a smooth stay, but it's just as important to remain flexible and adaptable when circumstances require it. While having guidelines in place helps avoid confusion, understanding that life doesn't always go according to plan can make a significant difference in the guest experience. For instance, if your guests request a late check-in due to travel delays or other unforeseen circumstances, consider offering a flexible solution, such as adjusting the check-in time or providing a self-check-in option. This thoughtful approach can go a long way in making your guests feel welcome and supported.

Flexibility extends to other areas as well. For example, if guests need to extend their stay or adjust their check-out time, accommodating their request when possible can lead to a more positive interaction. Being open to these adjustments not only demonstrates your hospitality but also shows that you're willing to go the extra mile to make their stay as stress-free and enjoyable as possible.

Incorporating flexibility into your guest experience, within reason, helps build goodwill and fosters positive relationships. By working with your guests when needed, you can turn a potentially stressful situation into an opportunity to exceed their expectations and create a lasting impression of excellent service.

Enforce the Rules

Enforcing your house rules consistently is crucial to maintaining a positive and respectful environment for all guests. Clear rules set the standard for expectations, and when they are violated, addressing the issue promptly and professionally is essential to protecting your space and ensuring that all future guests have a comfortable experience.

If a guest violates a rule, approach the situation with respect and clear communication. Start by calmly reminding the guest of the rule they have broken, whether it's related to noise, smoking, pets, or any other guideline you've established. If the violation is minor, you might issue a friendly reminder or request that they correct the issue. However, if the violation is more serious, such as hosting an unauthorized party or damaging property, you may need to take more immediate action.

In some cases, it may be necessary to charge a cleaning fee or additional charges to cover any damage or excessive mess caused by the violation. If the situation escalates and the guest's behavior is disruptive or unacceptable, you may need to ask them to leave. It's important to remain calm and professional during these interactions to avoid conflicts or negative reviews.

If the violation has impacted the guest experience or safety, consider leaving an honest and constructive review after their stay. Providing factual details about the situation in your review can help future hosts be aware of any potential issues. It's also essential to follow through with the house rules consistently to create a fair environment where all guests are held to the same standard.

Remember, upholding your house rules is not only about pro-tecting your space, but also about ensuring a positive experience for all guests, which helps maintain the reputation of your rental. By setting clear and reasonable house rules, you can help ensure that your guests have a comfortable and enjoyable stay in your space.

Chapter 11 Keeping Your Space Clean: How to Maintain a Clean and Tidy Home

One of the most important aspects of short-term vacation rental hosting is keeping your space clean and tidy. Guests expect a clean and comfortable space when they arrive, and maintaining a high standard of cleanliness is crucial for ensuring positive reviews and repeat business.

Develop a Cleaning Schedule

Creating a detailed cleaning schedule is essential for maintaining a consistently clean and welcoming space for your guests. A well-organized schedule ensures that your property is always in top condition and helps you stay on track with routine cleaning tasks.

Start by breaking down your cleaning schedule into daily,

weekly, and monthly tasks. For daily tasks, focus on the quick, high-touch areas that need regular attention to ensure a clean, fresh atmosphere for each guest. This includes sweeping or vacuuming floors, wiping down kitchen and bathroom surfaces, sanitizing light switches, door handles, and countertops, and ensuring that all common areas are tidy and free from clutter.

Weekly tasks should focus on deeper cleaning to maintain hygiene and comfort in your space. These tasks might include mopping floors, dusting furniture and shelves, vacuuming or washing rugs, deep cleaning the kitchen (such as cleaning the oven and refrigerator), and wiping down baseboards. It's also a good idea to clean and sanitize high-use appliances like the microwave and coffee maker.

Monthly tasks should include more thorough cleaning that might not be necessary as often but is still crucial for maintaining your space. This could involve washing windows, deep cleaning the bathroom (including scrubbing tiles and grout, cleaning showerheads, and sanitizing drains), washing and changing all bed linens and towels, and rotating or flipping mattresses. You should also clean light fixtures, ceiling fans, and air vents to maintain air quality.

By setting clear guidelines for each task, you'll ensure that all areas of your rental are attended to and that your guests experience a clean, comfortable environment throughout their stay. Having a consistent cleaning schedule in place will not only help maintain high cleanliness standards but also minimize last-minute stress and ensure that you're always ready for your next guest.

Provide Cleaning Supplies

It's essential to have a well-stocked inventory of cleaning supplies on hand to maintain your space in pristine condition before, during, and after each guest's stay. Make sure to have all the basic cleaning essentials readily available, such as a variety of cleaning solutions suited for different surfaces (like all-purpose cleaner, glass cleaner, disinfectant, and bathroom cleaner), sponges, scrub brushes, microfiber cloths, and paper towels. Ensure that you have a sufficient supply of disposable items, such as garbage bags and toilet paper, and stock up on any other specific cleaning products based on your space's needs, like specialty floor cleaners or upholstery spray.

In addition to having cleaning supplies for your own use, it can be helpful to provide some basic cleaning tools for your guests, ensuring they have the means to keep the space tidy during their stay. This might include a broom and dustpan, a handheld vacuum, a mop with a bucket, or a small cleaning caddy with essential items like multi-surface wipes, a dishwashing sponge, and a toilet brush. By offering these supplies, you give guests the flexibility to address any messes quickly and efficiently, helping them feel more comfortable and reducing the need for frequent requests for assistance.

Having the right supplies on hand for both your use and your guests' convenience ensures that your space remains in top con- dition and enhances the overall guest experience, encouraging positive reviews and repeat bookings.

Hire a Cleaning Service

If you find that cleaning your space yourself is too time-consuming or not a task you enjoy, hiring a professional cleaning service can be a highly effective solution. A professional cleaning team can ensure that your space is consistently spotless, thoroughly cleaned, and well-maintained between gueststays. They are equipped with the necessary tools, supplies, and expertise to handle every aspect of your space, including deep-cleaning tasks like sanitizing bathrooms, scrubbing kitchen appliances, dusting high-touch areas, and washing linens.

When selecting a cleaning service, it's important to choose a reputable company or independent cleaners who specialize in short-term vacation rental properties. A cleaning service that is familiar with the specific needs of rental properties will understand the importance of quick turnaround times, attention to detail, and ensuring a fresh, welcoming environment for each new guest. You can set up a schedule for regular cleanings be- tween check-ins or even after each guest's departure, depending on your booking frequency.

Hiring a professional cleaning service not only saves you valuable time but also helps maintain high standards of cleanliness, which is crucial for positive guest experiences. It can also help minimize the stress of last-minute bookings or guest check-ins, as you can rely on the cleaning service to keep your space in top condition and ready for visitors at all times. Additionally, a clean and well-maintained space can lead to higher ratings, better reviews, and increased bookings.

Inspect Your Space Regularly

Regularly inspecting your space is crucial to maintaining a high standard of cleanliness and ensuring that your property is always in top condition for your guests. Set aside time to thoroughly walk through your space at least once a week, or between guest stays, to check for any issues that might need attention. Look for common problem areas, such as stained or damaged linens, dirty bathroom fixtures, or worn-out furniture. Pay close attention to high-touch surfaces like door handles, light switches, and remote controls, which require frequent sanitization.

In addition to routine cleaning, inspect the overall condition of appliances, electronics, and furniture to make sure everything is functioning properly. Check for any maintenance issues such as leaks, broken light bulbs, or clogged drains. If you notice any items that need repair or replacement, address them promptly to avoid inconveniencing your guests. For example, if you find stained towels or bedding, replace them immediately with fresh linens to ensure a comfortable stay.

It's also a good idea to check the air quality, as well as the overall ambiance of your space. Ensure that the space is well-ventilated and that any lingering odors are addressed with air fresheners or natural remedies. By staying proactive in inspecting and addressing these areas, you'll help create a welcoming and comfortable environment for your guests. Timely attention to small details not only ensures cleanliness but also shows that you take pride in your property, which can lead to better reviews and repeat bookings.

Encourage Guests to Clean Up After Themselves

Encouraging your guests to clean up after themselves during their stay not only helps maintain the cleanliness of your space but also fosters a sense of responsibility and respect for your property. Start by providing clear and detailed instructions on how guests should dispose of their trash, including where to find trash bins, recycling containers, and any other disposal guidelines. Be sure to include specific instructions for separating recyclables, compostables, and general waste, as this can help your guests maintain an eco-friendly approach during their stay.

In addition to trash disposal, guide your guests on how to handle used linens, towels, and other items. Specify where they should place used towels, bed linens, or any other laundry items (e.g., in a designated laundry bin or in the bathroom) and let them know if they are expected to wash or strip the beds before check-out. If you prefer to handle laundry yourself, make sure this is clearly communicated.

Incorporate these expectations into your house rules, emphasizing the importance of keeping the space neat and tidy. Remind guests that maintaining a clean environment helps ensure that the next guest enjoys a pleasant and comfortable stay. You could also include a gentle reminder in your welcome guide or check- in message, outlining how small efforts from guests, such as wiping down surfaces or putting away dishes, can go a long way in helping keep your property in pristine condition.

Consider offering a few cleaning supplies like paper towels, dis-infectant wipes, and a broom or vacuum in an easily accessible location. This makes it easier for guests to quickly tidy up during their stay without feeling inconvenienced. By providing your guests with the tools and guidelines to maintain cleanliness, you'll promote a positive guest experience while preserving the condition of your space for future stays.

Chapter 12 Dealing with Issues: How to Handle Complaints and Problems

Even the best-run short-term rental listings will experience issues from time to time. Whether it's a complaint from a guest about a noisy neighbor or a maintenance issue that needs to be addressed, it's important to know how to handle these situations effectively. Here are some tips for dealing with issues:

Respond Promptly

When a guest brings an issue to your attention, it's essential to respond as quickly as possible to avoid escalating the situation. A timely response shows that you value their concerns and are committed to providing an exceptional experience. Begin by acknowledging the issue and expressing empathy, making sure the guest feels heard and understood. For example, you could say, "I'm really sorry to hear about the inconvenience you're experiencing. I understand how frustrating that must be."

Once you've acknowledged the concern, reassure the guest that you're actively taking steps to resolve it. Whether it involves troubleshooting an issue with the Wi-Fi, coordinating a maintenance request, or offering an alternative solution, clearly communicate the actions you're taking and provide an estimated timeline for when they can expect the issue to be addressed. If possible, offer an immediate temporary fix to make the guest feel more comfortable while the issue is being resolved.

For example, if the air conditioning isn't working, you could explain, "I've contacted our repair service, and they will be here within the next hour. In the meantime, I've brought you some fans to help with the temperature." This provides a sense of urgency and reassures the guest that you are actively working to resolve the problem.

If the issue requires more time to address, continue to keep the guest updated regularly. This ongoing communication shows that you are dedicated to making their stay as pleasant as possible, even when unexpected problems arise. In case of a more serious problem, such as a water leak or electrical failure, consider offering a partial refund, a discount, or a small gesture of goodwill to demonstrate your commitment to customer satisfaction.

By addressing issues promptly, communicating effectively, and showing a genuine willingness to resolve problems, you can often turn a negative experience into a positive one, enhancing guest satisfaction and encouraging repeat bookings.

Listen to the Guest

When a guest presents a complaint or issue, it's crucial to listen attentively and give them your full focus. Avoid interrupting them, and let them explain the situation in its entirety. By actively listening, you show that you value their feedback and are committed to understanding their perspective. Take the time to ask follow-up questions if necessary, to gain clarity on their concerns and ensure that you fully comprehend the problem. This helps you address their needs more effectively.

As you listen, show genuine empathy. Acknowledge the guest's feelings by validating their experience. For example, you could say, "I can imagine how frustrating that must be, and I'm really sorry that this has impacted your stay." Empathizing with their situation not only makes the guest feel heard but also demonstrates your commitment to providing a high level of hospitality, even when things go wrong.

By making it clear that you're genuinely taking their concerns seriously, you can defuse any frustration and prevent the situation from escalating into a more negative experience. Reassure the guest that you're focused on resolving the issue as quickly and effectively as possible. Let them know you appreciate their patience and understanding, and emphasize your commitment to ensuring their comfort.

In many cases, when a guest feels understood and supported, it can help to calm their emotions and foster a positive resolution. Your responsiveness and empathetic approach can turn an unpleasant situation into an opportunity to strengthen the guest relationship and enhance their overall experience.

Take Action to Resolve the Issue

Once a guest brings an issue to your attention, it's essential to act quickly to resolve it. If the problem is something you can fix yourself, such as a malfunctioning appliance, take immediate steps to address it. For example, if a kitchen appliance stops working, attempt to troubleshoot the issue or offer a replacement appliance if available. In cases where the problem requires technical expertise, such as plumbing issues or electrical faults, arrange for a professional repair service as soon as possible. Make sure to communicate with the guest about the steps you're taking and provide them with a timeline for when they can expect the issue to be resolved.

If the issue is beyond your control or requires external assistance, such as a noisy neighbor, reach out to the appropriate parties right away. Contact the building management, security, or local authorities if necessary, and inform your guest of the actions you're taking. Be proactive in following up to ensure that the problem is being addressed in a timely manner. For example, if you've contacted a neighbor about excessive noise, let your guest know that you are waiting for a response or have already spoken with the neighbor to resolve the issue.

In addition to taking action, always keep the guest informed of any progress. If an issue will take longer than expected to resolve, such as waiting for an outside vendor, update the guest regularly. Being transparent and keeping communication open can help reassure the guest that you're dedicated to making their stay as comfortable as possible, even if issues arise.

Offer a Solution

When a guest expresses a problem or complaint, it's important to offer a thoughtful and fair solution to address their concerns. The solution will vary depending on the nature and severity of the issue, but it should always be something that demonstrates your commitment to providing excellent customer service and ensuring their satisfaction.

For example, if the guest experienced inconveniences due to maintenance issues, such as a broken appliance or air conditioning failure, you may offer them a partial discount for the inconvenience or a voucher for a future stay. If the issue is more significant, such as a disturbance from neighboring properties, you may consider offering a free night or an upgrade to a better room or unit if available. In some cases, offering a gesture such as complimentary snacks, drinks, or a local gift basket may help demonstrate that you care about their experience.

It's also essential to communicate your solution clearly and professionally. Let the guest know exactly what you're offering, why you're providing it, and how it will resolve the issue. Ensure that your solution is framed as a goodwill gesture to maintain the positive relationship with the guest.

Finally, once the solution has been proposed, ask the guest

if they are satisfied with the outcome. Check in with them to ensure that they feel their concerns have been addressed appropriately. If the guest is still dissatisfied, be open to additional suggestions or accommodations to improve their experience. By going the extra mile and ensuring your guest's satisfaction, you show that you're dedicated to maintaining a positive and professional relationship, even when challenges arise.

Follow Up

Once the issue has been resolved, it's important to follow up with your guest to ensure they are satisfied with the solution and their overall experience. This follow-up demonstrates your commitment to providing excellent customer service and helps to rebuild any trust that may have been affected by the initial problem.

Reach out to the guest via their preferred communication method—whether that's email, text, or through the booking platform—and politely inquire if everything is now to their satisfaction. Express genuine interest in their feedback, and ask if there's anything else you can do to enhance their stay. This not only shows that you care about their experience but also allows you to address any lingering concerns they may have, preventing small issues from escalating further.

If possible, ask if they feel the resolution met their expectations or if they would suggest any improvements. This can be an opportunity to reaffirm the positive aspects of their stay and to correct any minor lingering issues. It's important to keep the tone friendly, professional, and focused on ensuring their complete satisfaction.

Taking the time to follow up with guests can also help mitigate the likelihood of negative reviews. If they feel that their concerns were genuinely addressed and that they were valued as a guest, they are much more likely to leave a positive review, or even amend a prior negative comment. Demonstrating your commitment to guest satisfaction through consistent follow-up can turn a potentially negative experience into a lasting positive impression, strengthening your relationship with the guest and encouraging repeat visits.

The key is to respond promptly, listen to the guest, take action to resolve the issue, offer a solution, and follow up to ensure satisfaction.

Chapter 13 Upselling Your Space: How to Add Extra Value and Increase Your Earnings

As an short-term rental host, you can add extra value to your listing and increase your earnings in many ways. Here are some tips for upselling your space:

Offer Additional Services

Consider enhancing your guests' experience by offering a variety of additional services that can make their stay more convenient, enjoyable, and memorable. You could offer practical amenities such as a shuttle service to and from the airport, ensuring a seamless arrival and departure experience. If your area is known for outdoor activities, bike rentals or even guided tours can offer guests an opportunity to explore the local surroundings in a unique way. Additionally, providing a stocked fridge with snacks, drinks, or even breakfast essentials can save guests time and add a thoughtful touch to their stay.

Branded merchandise, such as mugs, tote bags, or T-shirts, can be a fun way to make your guests feel more connected to your space and offer them a souvenir to take home. Partnering with local businesses can further elevate your offering. For instance, you could collaborate with a nearby gym or pool to provide guests with access to fitness facilities, or offer discounts or exclusive deals at local restaurants, cafes, or attractions.

You might also want to consider organizing local experiences like wine tours, food tastings, or cultural excursions to introduce guests to the best your area has to offer. If your region has any seasonal events or unique activities, such as festivals, outdoor concerts, or hiking trails, you could provide curated packages for guests to enjoy.

These services not only enhance the guest experience but also set your property apart from the competition. By offering convenience, exclusive local experiences, and memorable touches, you make your listing more attractive to potential guests. Plus, these added services can lead to better reviews, increased guest satisfaction, and potentially higher booking rates, as travelers often seek properties that provide value beyond just the basics.

Provide Special Amenities

To ensure your guests feel truly pampered and comfortable during their stay, consider offering a range of special amenities that elevate their experience and provide a sense of luxury. Start by investing in high-quality, luxury bedding, including soft, crisp sheets, plush comforters, and a variety of pillows to ensure a restful night's sleep. You might also consider offering hypoallergenic or memory foam options to accommodate different guest preferences.

Enhance the bathroom experience with premium toiletries, such as high-end shampoos, conditioners, body wash, and lotions. Providing eco-friendly, cruelty-free, or locally sourced products can also appeal to environmentally conscious travelers and add a unique touch to your space. Soft, fluffy towels and bathrobes can further enhance the feeling of indulgence.

To make your guests' mornings even better, provide a selection of gourmet teas and freshly brewed coffee, along with a variety of creamer and sweeteners. You could also include a coffee maker or espresso machine, along with high-quality coffee beans or pods, to cater to different tastes and give guests the feeling of being in a café from the comfort of their own space.

Small touches like high-end candles, a cozy throw blanket on the couch, or a personalized welcome note can also add to the overall feeling of luxury and thoughtfulness. These extra amenities show your guests that you've gone above and beyond to ensure their stay is comfortable and memorable.

These thoughtful additions can make a significant difference in the guest experience, potentially leading to glowing reviews, positive word-of-mouth, and repeat bookings. By providing an elevated, comfortable, and personalized stay, you create an environment that encourages guests to return and recommend your property to others.

Highlight Unique Features

When creating your listing, it's essential to highlight any unique features or standout elements of your space that set it apart from other properties. This could include architectural details like a spacious rooftop terrace that offers sweeping city views or a cozy balcony perfect for morning coffee. A breathtaking view, whether it's of a serene lake, rolling mountains, or a vibrant skyline, can be a major selling point, so be sure to capture this in both the description and photos to make it impossible for guests to overlook.

If your property boasts high-end or custom finishes, such as a designer kitchen with premium appliances, marble countertops, or a professional-grade stove, these features should be prominently featured in your listing. A well-appointed kitchen can appeal to guests who love to cook or those looking to entertain, making it a key selling point for longer stays or those in need of a fully equipped space.

Additionally, if your home has any other exceptional elements, such as a private pool, hot tub, or fireplace, or offers high-tech amenities like smart home features or a high-quality sound system, be sure to mention these in your description. Unique design elements like exposed brick walls, vaulted ceilings, or eco-friendly features such as solar panels can also be strong selling points that attract specific types of guests.

By showcasing the distinctive features of your property in your listing, you not only enhance its appeal but also increase the perceived value, potentially allowing you to charge a premium price. Including high-quality photos that capture these features in their best light can further elevate your listing, helping you attract guests who are specifically looking for those special touches and are willing to pay more for the experience.

Offer Special Packages

Consider offering thoughtfully curated special packages designed to enhance your guests' experience and make their stay truly memorable. These packages can cater to various types of travelers and help set your listing apart from others, attracting guests who are seeking a more personalized or unique stay.

For example, a romantic weekend getaway package could include features like a bottle of wine or champagne upon arrival, a bouquet of fresh flowers, candles, and perhaps a gift card to a local fine dining restaurant. You could also offer add- ons such as a couples' massage or a private chef experience to elevate the romantic experience. Such packages create a memorable, all-inclusive experience for couples and encourage longer stays, particularly for anniversaries, honeymoons, or special celebrations.

For family-friendly packages, consider providing a range of activities that cater to all age groups. This could include board games, a selection of kids' books or toys, a family movie night setup with popcorn, or passes for nearby family attractions such as a zoo, amusement park, or children's museum. You could also offer essential amenities such as baby monitors, cribs, high chairs, or strollers to make traveling with young children more convenient. Packages like these not only appeal to families looking for a stress-free vacation but also help attract repeat bookings from guests who are looking for value and convenience during their stay.

Additionally, you could tailor your offerings to specific themes or occasions, such as a wellness retreat with yoga mats, spa products, healthy snacks, and access to nearby hiking or meditation spots, or a holiday-themed package complete with festive decorations, seasonal treats, and a guided tour of local holiday events or markets. These types of special packages give your guests a unique experience they can't easily find elsewhere and encourage them to choose your listing over others.

By offering these distinctive packages, you not only enhance your property's appeal but also create a more memorable and personalized experience that increases guest satisfaction, generates positive reviews, and encourages repeat bookings. These packages can also serve as an additional revenue stream, further boosting your rental income.

By incorporating these tips into your listing, you can add extra value and increase your earnings as an short-term vacation rental host. Remember to always communicate the additional services and amenities that you offer in your listing description and ensure that they're reflected in your pricing.

Chapter 14 Getting Positive Reviews: How to Encourage Happy Guests to Leave Great Reviews

Positive reviews are crucial to the success of your short-term vacation rental listing. They can help you attract more guests, increase occupancy, and command a higher price.

Provide Excellent Service

The most effective way to ensure positive reviews is by consistently providing exceptional service that leaves a lasting impression on your guests. Begin by creating a warm and welcoming environment from the moment they arrive, ensuring they feel valued and at home. This includes offering a thorough and friendly check-in process, where you personally greet them or provide clear, easy-to-follow instructions if you're not available. Take the time to ask if they need anything upon arrival, and ensure the space is spotless, well-stocked, and prepared with thoughtful touches such as fresh flowers, local treats, or a handwritten welcome note.

Throughout their stay, prioritize guest comfort and satisfaction by being attentive and responsive. Respond promptly to any inquiries or concerns, whether it's about the Wi-Fi password, local recommendations, or any issues within the property. Aim to resolve any problems quickly and efficiently, showing that you genuinely care about their experience. If a guest requests additional amenities, such as extra towels or help with a particular issue, do your best to accommodate them immediately.

Go the extra mile by anticipating their needs. For example, if you know the weather is going to be particularly hot or cold, provide them with extra fans or blankets without them needing to ask. If you're aware of any special occasions during their stay, such as an anniversary or birthday, consider surprising them with a small thoughtful gesture like a bottle of wine, a custom gift, or a discount on a future stay.

It's important to also follow up during their stay to make sure everything is going smoothly. A simple message asking if they need anything or if everything is to their satisfaction can go a long way in building rapport and addressing any issues before they escalate.

By consistently exceeding expectations—whether it's through communication, convenience, or thoughtful details—you not only create a positive experience that your guests will remember, but also inspire them to leave glowing reviews. Positive reviews stem from an authentic, personalized approach to hospitality that makes guests feel like they are more than just customers— they are valued individuals whose comfort and happiness are your top priority.

Communicate Clearly

Clear and effective communication is essential for creating a seamless and positive experience for your guests. From the moment they book their stay, ensure that they have all the information they need to feel confident and prepared. Provide comprehensive details about your listing, including a detailed description of the property, amenities, and any unique features that will enhance their stay. Include clear check-in and check-out instructions, specifying the exact time, method of entry (whether it's a key lockbox, smart lock, or in-person check-in), and any special procedures they may need to follow.

Make sure to outline your house rules in a straightforward and concise manner, covering important aspects like noise levels, smoking policies, pet rules, and the handling of trash. Also, include any information about additional services or amenities that could elevate their stay, such as local transportation options, parking instructions, access to shared facilities (like a pool or gym), or available extras like bike rentals or grocery delivery.

In addition to the pre-arrival details, maintain open communication throughout their stay. Respond to any messages or inquiries promptly, ideally within an hour, and be proactive in addressing potential concerns or providing assistance as needed. Whether it's recommending local attractions, helping them troubleshoot an appliance issue, or simply checking in to ensure they're comfortable, your availability and attentiveness are key to building trust and fostering a positive relationship with your guests.

Consider sending a personalized message before their arrival with all the necessary information, and offer to assist them with any special requests or requirements. If they reach out during their stay with questions or issues, aim to respond as quickly as possible, providing clear and friendly solutions. Make sure they know how to contact you, whether it's via phone, email, or the messaging system on your booking platform, and reassure them that you are just a message or phone call away.

By consistently maintaining clear, responsive, and helpful communication, you demonstrate a commitment to making your guests' experience enjoyable and hassle-free. This proactive approach not only ensures that they have all the information they need but also fosters a sense of trust and hospitality that can lead to glowing reviews and repeat bookings.

Ask for Feedback

After your guests check out, proactively request their feedback to gain valuable insights into their experience. You can ask them to share their thoughts through the short-term rental messaging system, or send a follow-up review request email that expresses your appreciation for their stay and encourages them to provide honest feedback. Make it clear that their opinion matters and that you're committed to continually improving the guest experience.

In your message, consider including specific questions to guide their feedback, such as:

· What did you enjoy most about your stay?
· Was there anything that could have been improved or made your experience more comfortable?
· Did you have any challenges or issues during your stay that we should address?

Encourage them to provide both positive comments and constructive criticism. By doing so, you demonstrate that you're open to all kinds of feedback and committed to making necessary adjustments to enhance future guests' experiences.

When requesting reviews, emphasize that their honest opinions help you to refine and improve your services. Show appreciation for any suggestions or critiques they offer and let them know you are grateful for their time in sharing their thoughts. This can be done in a friendly, thoughtful manner, making sure to express your genuine desire to provide the best possible experience for future guests.

Be sure to respond to any feedback you receive, especially if a guest has raised a concern. Thank them for their input and outline any steps you plan to take to address issues or improve upon the areas they've mentioned. By acknowledging their feedback and showing a commitment to making improvements, you can turn any negative comments into an opportunity to build trust with your guests and refine your listing.

Implementing feedback from guests not only helps you create a better experience for future stays, but it also shows potential guests that you value input and are always working to improve your offering. This continuous cycle of feedback and improvement can lead to higher guest satisfaction, positive reviews, and increased bookings.

Follow Up with a Thank-You Message

After your guests check out, take the opportunity to send a thoughtful follow-up thank-you message to express your appreciation for their stay. This can be done via the short-term rental messaging system or, if you're sending a formal review request, through a dedicated thank-you email. In your message, sincerely thank them for choosing your property and for trusting you with their stay. Personalize the message by referencing something specific from their time with you, such as a positive interaction or a memorable moment during their stay, to make the note feel more personal.

In addition to your thanks, kindly encourage them to leave a review. Politely ask them to share their thoughts and experiences to help future guests make informed decisions. If appropriate, you can also remind them of the review process and how it contributes to maintaining and improving your listing.

You can phrase it something like this:

"Thank you so much for choosing to stay at [Property Name]. It was a pleasure hosting you, and I hope you had a wonderful time! Your feedback is incredibly valuable, and I'd appreciate it if you could take a few minutes to leave a review of your stay. It helps me continue providing a top-notch experience for future guests. If you have any suggestions or things I can improve upon, feel free to share those as well."

This follow-up message should convey both your gratitude and your commitment to continually enhancing the guest experience. Make sure to express that you're open to feedback and eager to ensure future stays are just as enjoyable. By sending a thank-you message and encouraging reviews, you not only foster goodwill with your guests but also help build your reputation and attract more bookings..

Chapter 15 Managing Your Finances: How to Track Your Income and Expenses

Managing your finances is an important aspect of short-term rental hosting. Keeping track of your income and expenses can help you understand your profitability and make informed decisions about your listing.

Keep Detailed Records

It is crucial to maintain comprehensive and organized records of all income and expenses related to your short-term vacation rental listing to ensure the financial success and long-term sustainability of your business. This includes not only your rental income but also additional sources of revenue, such as cleaning fees, booking fees, and any special service charges you may offer. On the expense side, make sure to document every cost, including but not limited to:

• Property Maintenance and Repairs: Regular upkeep such as plumbing, electrical work, HVAC servicing, lawn care, or pest control.

• Cleaning Costs: Fees paid to cleaners, supplies purchased, and any other cleaning-related expenses (including cleaning products or professional deep cleaning services).

• Utilities: Utility bills like electricity, water, internet, heating/cooling, and any other necessary utilities.

• Property Taxes and Insurance: Any insurance premiums, property taxes, or other government-required fees.

• Marketing and Advertising: Costs associated with promoting your listing, such as paid ads on booking platforms, professional photography, or website hosting fees if applicable.

• Supplies and Amenities: Regular purchases for guest amenities (toiletries, linens, kitchenware, etc.), as well as any replacement or upgrade costs for furniture or appliances.

• Management Fees: If you use a property management service or pay someone to handle bookings and guest communication, document these fees as well.

• Other Miscellaneous Expenses: Any additional costs associated with your short-term rental, like licensing fees, cleaning products, and upgrades to enhance the guest experience (such as new tech, furniture, or decor).

By keeping a meticulous record of all these financial elements, you will be able to accurately assess your profitability, track seasonal income fluctuations, and identify trends in your expenses. This information will also be valuable when it comes to tax time, as it will help you ensure compliance with tax laws and maximize eligible deductions.

Moreover, detailed record-keeping helps you identify areas where you can cut costs (such as switching service providers or reducing utility usage) or boost revenue (by adjusting pricing, adding new services, or offering discounts). By reviewing your financial records regularly, you can make more informed decisions, optimize your operations, and ultimately improve the financial performance of your short-term rental business.

Set Aside Money for Taxes

As a short-term rental host, it is essential to understand that you are legally responsible for paying taxes on the rental income you generate. This includes income from the booking fees, cleaning fees, and any additional services you charge for, such as transportation, amenities, or special packages. To avoid surprises at tax time, it's important to proactively set aside a portion of your earnings for taxes throughout the year. A common rule of thumb is to allocate 25-30% of your rental income for federal, state, and local taxes, but this may vary depending on your tax bracket and location.

Additionally, keeping track of all deductible expenses related to your rental property is crucial, as these can help reduce your overall tax liability. Deductible expenses can include:

• Operating Expenses: Costs such as cleaning services, maintenance, utilities (electricity, water, internet), and property management fees.

• Property-related Expenses: Items like repairs, property

taxes, homeowner's insurance, mortgage interest, and depreciation.

• Supplies and Amenities: Expenses for toiletries, linens, kitchen supplies, and any upgrades or improvements made to the property.

• Advertising and Marketing: Costs related to promoting your rental on platforms such as Airbnb, Vrbo, or your own website, as well as photography or listing fees.

• Travel Expenses: If you need to travel for property-related reasons, such as inspecting the property or purchasing supplies, you may be able to deduct those expenses as well.

It's crucial to maintain detailed records and receipts of all these expenses so you can accurately report them during tax filing. Consider using accounting software designed for rental property owners to track income and expenses automatically.

Given the complexity of short-term rental tax laws, which can vary by state or even city, it's a wise decision to consult with a tax professional or accountant who specializes in rental properties. A tax expert can guide you through the intricacies of local tax laws, ensure that you're complying with all regulations, and help you identify deductions or credits that you may be eligible for. By working with a professional, you can minimize your tax burden, avoid penalties, and ensure that you are fully compliant with the applicable tax codes.

Use Accounting Software

Using accounting software is a highly effective way to streamline and manage your finances as a short-term rental host. These software programs offer a wide range of tools designed to help you keep track of your income, expenses, and other financial activities, allowing you to stay organized and avoid any potential financial mismanagement. Many accounting software solutions are specifically tailored to the needs of short-term rental hosts and can seamlessly integrate with popular booking platforms like Airbnb, Vrbo, and Booking.com. This integration allows the software to automatically import and categorize transactions, making it easy to track your rental income, cleaning fees, service charges, and other payments without manual entry.

In addition to tracking income and expenses, accounting software often includes features that help you manage your cash flow, monitor payments, and plan for taxes. For example, you can set up automated expense categories for costs such as utilities, maintenance, property management, or supplies, ensuring that your financial records are both accurate and complete. You can also set reminders for upcoming payments, such as property taxes or bills, to help ensure that you never miss an important deadline.

One of the biggest advantages of using accounting software is its ability to generate detailed financial reports. These reports can include:

• Profit and Loss Statements: These summarize your total income and expenses over a specific period, giving you an overview of your profitability. By regularly reviewing your profit and loss statements, you can spot trends and identify areas where you might need to reduce costs or increase revenue.

• Balance Sheets: A balance sheet provides a snapshot of your financial position by detailing your assets, liabilities, and equity at a given point in time. This is particularly helpful for understanding your overall financial health and planning for the future.

• Cash Flow Statements: These reports show how money is flowing in and out of your business, helping you assess your liquidity and ability to cover operating expenses.

• Tax Reports: Some accounting software can automatically generate tax reports that summarize deductible expenses, making tax season much less stressful and ensuring you are taking full advantage of all available deductions.

The ability to quickly generate and analyze these reports helps you make informed financial decisions, optimize your rental business's operations, and ensure that your listing remains profitable in the long term. Additionally, by using accounting software, you can easily share financial records with your accountant or tax professional, making tax filing and financial planning a smoother process.

Monitor Your Profitability

Monitoring your profitability is crucial to the long-term success and sustainability of your short-term rental listing. By consistently tracking both your income and expenses, you can accurately determine your net profit and gain a clear understanding of your financial performance. This process involves not only reviewing your rental income, such as nightly rates, cleaning fees, and any additional charges, but also keeping a detailed record of all your operating costs. These might include expenses like utilities, maintenance, property management fees, insurance premiums, property taxes, and any marketing or advertising costs. By carefully categorizing and monitoring these financial flows, you'll be able to identify both profitable areas and those where you may be overspending.

Once you have a clear picture of your revenue and expenses, you can calculate your net profit by subtracting your total costs from your total income. This will give you an accurate reflection of your profitability, enabling you to make data-driven decisions about pricing, spending, and investment. If your costs are outweighing your income, you'll be able to identify specific areas where you may need to make adjustments, such as reducing operational expenses, optimizing pricing strategies, or cutting back on unnecessary services or amenities.

Additionally, comparing your financial performance to that of other similar listings in your area can provide valuable insights into how competitive your pricing is and how efficiently you're managing your property. Many short-term vacation rental platforms and third-party tools offer market analysis features that allow you to benchmark your listing against local competitors. By understanding where your listing stands in terms of nightly rates, occupancy rates, and overall profitability, you can identify opportunities for improvement. This comparison helps you determine if you're underpricing, overpricing, or offering services that others may not, giving you a competitive edge.

For example, if your occupancy rate is lower than the average for your area, you may need to consider adjusting your pricing or enhancing your marketing efforts to attract more guests. On the other hand, if your listing is outperforming similar properties in terms of revenue, you can evaluate the factors that are driving that success, such as superior guest reviews, premium amenities, or an ideal location. Ultimately, tracking and comparing your financial performance helps ensure that you are maximizing your potential earnings and optimizing the operation of your short-term rental.

Adjust Your Pricing

If you find that your short-term rental listing isn't as profitable as you'd like, adjusting your pricing strategy can be a key solution. Start by analyzing your current pricing structure and assessing whether it aligns with market trends, the demand in your area, and the amenities you offer. One effective approach is to adjust your rates seasonally. For instance, during peak seasons, holidays, or special events (such as festivals, conferences, or local celebrations), you can raise your nightly rates to capitalize on the higher demand. Conversely, during off-peak periods, when demand is lower, you might consider lowering your rates to attract more guests and increase bookings.

Additionally, you can experiment with dynamic pricing strategies, where your rates fluctuate in real time based on factors like local demand, competition, and booking patterns. There are pricing tools and software available that can help automate this process by adjusting your rates for you based on factors such as occupancy rates in your area or competitor pricing. This can help ensure that you're pricing your listing optimally without leaving money on the table or pricing yourself out of the market.

When adjusting your pricing, it's essential to carefully track the results to understand how the changes impact your occupancy rates, booking frequency, and overall profitability. Use analytics tools to monitor these metrics over time and adjust your strategy accordingly. For example, if you raise your rates during a busy season and notice that your occupancy rate drops significantly, it may indicate that your price point is too high for potential guests. On the other hand, if you lower your rates during a slow period and see an increase in bookings, it may suggest that you've struck the right balance between price and demand.

It's also a good idea to periodically review competitor pricing in your area to ensure that your rates remain competitive. If similar properties are offering comparable amenities at lower rates, it might be necessary to adjust your pricing to stay competitive, especially if you're struggling with occupancy.

Furthermore, regularly assessing guest feedback and reviews can provide insight into whether guests perceive your rates as offering good value relative to the experience they receive.

Finally, consider offering discounts or special promotions for longer stays or early bookings to encourage guests to book ahead of time. For example, offering a discount for bookings of seven nights or more can help boost occupancy during slower periods, while offering early bird promotions can incentivize potential guests to commit to their stay sooner. By carefully monitoring how these pricing adjustments impact your business, you'll be able to fine-tune your strategy to maximize both occupancy and profitability.

Chapter 16 Conclusion: Recap and Next Steps for Successful Hosting

Congratulations! You've completed *Revenue Rise for Rentals: A Complete Guide to Growing Your Short-Term Rental Property Business.* By now, you should feel equipped with the knowledge and tools to build and grow a successful short-term rental business, while providing a fantastic experience for your guests.

Let's take a moment to recap the key points covered in this guide and outline the next steps on your path to becoming a thriving host.

We started with the fundamentals of hosting, examining the rising popularity of short-term rentals and why this market offers such exciting opportunities. We then discussed the essential steps to get your listing live—from creating your account and setting up your space to ensuring it's guest-ready. With your property prepared, we explored critical aspects like crafting an effective pricing strategy, writing compelling descriptions, and best practices for clear, engaging guest communication.

We also learned about the logistics of booking management, including how to handle reservations and cancellations, provide a seamless check-in process, and establish house rules that ensure your space is treated with care. Maintaining a clean, welcoming space and addressing guest concerns promptly were also key focus areas to help you maintain positive reviews and repeat bookings.

From there, we shifted to ways to increase your earnings, from upselling additional services to leveraging positive guest reviews. We wrapped up the guide by diving into financial management—tracking your income, managing expenses, and keeping detailed records to help you assess your profitability and make informed business decisions.

Here are some of the essential takeaways to remember from this guide:

· Building a successful short-term vacation rental listing requires thoughtful planning, from preparing your property to crafting a clear, engaging listing.
· Effective communication with your guests is the foundation of an exceptional guest experience.
· Properly managing bookings, maintaining a clean, welcoming home, and addressing concerns quickly are key to ensuring happy guests and positive reviews.
· Upselling services and encouraging guests to leave reviews can significantly boost your earnings.

• Keeping detailed financial records allows you to track performance, optimize profitability, and make data-driven decisions.

With these strategies and insights, you're well on your way to hosting success! The next step is to put these ideas into action. Test out different pricing models, experiment with additional services, and most importantly, continue to prioritize your guests' experience. By listening to feedback and staying open to adjusting your approach, you can continually improve your listing and elevate your hosting business.

Hosting is a journey of continuous learning and improvement. The more you refine your processes and adapt to guest needs, the more your rental property will stand out in a competitive market.

Thank you for reading *Revenue Rise for Rentals.* I'm excited for you as you embark on your hosting journey, and I wish you great success in your rental business! May your efforts lead to a steady rise in revenue, glowing guest reviews, and a rewarding and profitable venture.

Bonus
Material

Real Estate Investing Common Terms and Definitions

A

Absorption Rate - The rate at which available properties are sold in a specific market during a given time.

Adjustable-Rate Mortgage (ARM) - A mortgage with an interest rate that changes periodically based on a benchmark.

Amortization - The gradual repayment of a loan over time through scheduled payments.

Appraisal - A professional evaluation of a property's market value

Asset Class - A group of investments with similar characteristics, such as residential or commercial real estate.

B

BRRRR Strategy - Buy, Rehab, Rent, Refinance, Repeat; a popular real estate investment strategy.

Balloon Payment - A large payment due at the end of a loan term.

Basis Point - A unit of measure for interest rate changes, equal to 0.01%.

C

CapEx (Capital Expenditures) - Funds used to improve or maintain a property.

Capital Gains - The profit earned from selling a property for more than its purchase price.

Cash Flow - The net income generated by a property after expenses.

Closing Costs - Fees and expenses incurred during the purchase or sale of a property.

Collateral - An asset used to secure a loan.

Comparative Market Analysis (CMA) - An analysis of comparable properties to estimate a property's value.

Conventional Loan - A mortgage not insured by a government agency.

D

Debt Service Coverage Ratio (DSCR) - A metric to assess a property's ability to cover its loan payments.

Deed - A legal document that transfers ownership of a property.

Depreciation - A decrease in a property's value over time for tax purposes.

Down Payment - The initial cash payment made when purchasing a property.

Due Diligence - The process of researching a property before purchase.

E

Equity - The difference between a property's market value and the amount owed on it.

Escrow - A third-party account that holds funds during a transaction.

Exit Strategy - A plan for selling or disposing of an investment property.

Expense Ratio - A metric that shows the operating expenses relative to income.

Exclusive Right to Sell - A listing agreement where the agent receives commission regardless of who sells the property.

F

Fair Market Value (FMV) - The price a property would sell for under normal market conditions.

FHA Loan - A government-backed loan with lower down payment requirements.

Fix-and-Flip - A strategy of buying, renovating, and selling properties for a profit.

Foreclosure - The legal process of repossessing a property due to loan default.

Functional Obsolescence - A property's reduced value due to outdated features.

G

Gross Rent Multiplier (GRM) - A metric to evaluate the profitability of a rental property.

Guarantor - A person or entity that guarantees loan repayment.

Ground Lease - A lease agreement for the land on which a property is built.

Grant Deed - A document transferring property ownership with guarantees against prior claims.

Gross Income - The total income generated by a property before expenses.

H

Hard Money Loan - A short-term loan secured by real estate.

HOA (Homeowners Association) - An organization managing a community's common areas.

Home Equity Loan - A loan secured by the equity in a property.

House Hacking - Living in one part of a property while renting out others.

HUD (Housing and Urban Development) - A U.S. government agency focused on housing policies.

I

Income Property - Real estate purchased primarily for income generation.

Inspection Contingency - A clause allowing buyers to back out if the property fails inspection.

Interest Rate - The cost of borrowing money, expressed as a percentage.

Investment Property - Real estate purchased for financial return.

Inventory - The total number of properties available in a market.

J

Joint Tenancy - A form of property ownership shared by two or more parties.

Judgment Lien - A legal claim on a property due to a court judgment.

Jumbo Loan - A mortgage that exceeds conventional loan limits.

Just Cause Eviction - Laws requiring landlords to provide a valid reason for eviction.

Judicial Foreclosure - A foreclosure process requiring court involvement.

K

Key Money - A payment made to secure a lease or rental agreement.

Kick-Out Clause - A provision allowing sellers to accept another offer if the buyer fails to meet contingencies.

Kitchen Upgrade - Renovations in the kitchen to increase property value.

Knockdown - A property intended for demolition and redevelopment.

Knowledgeable Agent - A real estate professional with

expertise in a specific market.

L

Landlord - The owner of a rental property.

Lease Agreement - A contract between landlord and tenant outlining terms.

Lien - A legal claim on a property as security for a debt.

Loan-to-Value Ratio (LTV) - A metric showing the loan amount relative to property value.

Location Analysis - Evaluating a property's location for investment potential.

M

Market Value - The price a property would fetch in an open market.

Mortgage - A loan used to purchase real estate.

Multifamily Property - A property with multiple residential units.

Maintenance Costs - Expenses for maintaining a property's condition.

Management Fees - Charges for professional property management services.

N

Net Operating Income (NOI) - The income from a property after operating expenses.

Non-Recourse Loan - A loan where the lender can only claim the collateral.

Notice to Vacate - A notice to a tenant to leave the property.

Negative Cash Flow - When property expenses exceed income.

Neighborhood Watch - A community program for property safety.

O

Occupancy Rate - The percentage of occupied units in a property.

Operating Expenses - Costs incurred to run and maintain a property.

Owner Financing - A financing arrangement where the seller provides the loan.

Option Agreement - A contract giving the right to buy a property at a future date.

Off-Market Property - A property not listed publicly for sale.

P

Passive Income - Earnings from rental properties with minimal effort.

Pre-Approval - A lender's estimate of how much a buyer can borrow.

Principal - The original loan amount.

Property Tax - Taxes levied on real estate by local governments.

Property Manager - A professional who manages a rental property on behalf of the owner.

Q

Quitclaim Deed - A document transferring property ownership without guarantees.

Qualified Tenant - A renter meeting the landlord's screening criteria.

Quarterly Revenue - Income earned from a property in a three-month period.

Quiet Title Action - A lawsuit to resolve property ownership disputes.

Quality of Life - A factor affecting a property's desirability.

R

Return on Investment (ROI) - A measure of the profitability of an investment.

Rental Agreement - A contract specifying rental terms.

Real Estate Agent - A professional facilitating property transactions.

REIT (Real Estate Investment Trust) - A company owning or financing income-generating properties.

Rehabilitation Loan - A loan for property renovation.

S

Section 8 Housing - Government-subsidized rental housing for low-income tenants.

Seller Financing - Financing provided by the seller to the buyer.

Single-Family Home - A property designed for one family.

Short Sale - A property sale for less than the amount owed on the mortgage.

Survey - A professional assessment of property boundaries and features.

T

Tenant Screening - The process of evaluating potential renters.

Title Insurance - Insurance protecting against property owner-ship disputes.

Turnkey Property - A property ready for immediate rental or occupancy.

Tax Benefits - Deductions or incentives available to property owners.

Triple Net Lease (NNN) – A lease where the tenant pays property taxes, insurance, and maintenance.

More Hosting Resources

Property Management Tools

- Guesty: Comprehensive property management software offering booking management, automated messaging, and team coordination.

- Hostfully: A property management platform that includes guest communication, channel management, and digital guidebooks.

- Lodgify: Allows hosts to create a custom rental website, manage bookings, and integrate with major platforms like Airbnb and VRBO.

- Hospitable (formerly Smartbnb): Automates guest messaging, task scheduling, and calendar syncing.

Pricing and Revenue Management

- Pricelabs: Dynamic pricing tool that adjusts rates based on market trends, demand, and local events.
- Beyond Pricing: Revenue management platform to optimize nightly rates and maximize profitability.
- Wheelhouse: Offers customizable pricing strategies and market insights to help hosts maximize earnings.

Cleaning and Maintenance Management

- TurnoverBnB: Automates cleaning schedules, connects with professional cleaners, and integrates with booking platforms.

- Properly: Visual cleaning checklists and quality control tool to ensure cleaning standards are met.
- Handy: On-demand home cleaning and maintenance services for short-term rentals.

Guest Experience Enhancement

- Airbnb Experiences: Offer local experiences to your guests to enhance their stay.
- Touch Stay: Create digital guest guidebooks with property details, local recommendations, and check-in/out instructions.
- Welcome: Helps hosts curate personalized travel recommendations for guests.

Communication and Messaging

- WhatsAppBusiness: Easily communicate with guests using automated replies and quick responses.
- Slack: Useful for coordinating with your cleaning team or co-hosts.
- Tidio: Chatbot and live chat tool to provide quick responses to guest inquiries.

Marketing and Branding

- Canva: Design marketing materials like listing images, social media posts, and brochures.
- Mailchimp: Build email campaigns to stay connected with previous guests and promote special offers.
- Later: Schedule and manage social media content to attract potential guests.

Legal and Financial Management

- TurboTax: Tax preparation software tailored for short-term rental income.
- Gusto: Payroll and financial management tool for hosts employing cleaners or other staff.
- Avail: Tenant and property management software that includes legal document templates.

Insurance and Security

- Proper Insurance: Offers comprehensive coverage for short-term rental properties.
- Safely: Provides short-term rental insurance and guest screening services.
- Minut: Monitor noise levels to ensure compliance with local regulations and maintain good relationships with neighbors.

Learning and Community

- Airbnb Host Community: Join forums to exchange tips and advice with other hosts.
- BiggerPockets: Short-Term Rentals: A hub for real estate investors and hosts to share insights.
- YouTubeChannels:: Check out channels like *The Short-Term Show or Rental Recon for actionable tips.*

AdditionalToolsandServices

- Keycafe: Secure key exchange system for guest check-in.
- Nest: Smart thermostats and cameras for property monitoring and energy efficiency.
- iGMS: Centralized platform for managing bookings, reviews, and team tasks.

These resources will help you streamline operations, enhance guest experiences, and maximize profitability as a short-term vacation rental host.

Also by Amanda Otis

Discover valuable resources for real estate investors and short-term rental hosts who want to increase profits and grow a successful business. Each book in this series offers expert strategies, practical tips, and clear step-by-step guidance to help you improve your properties, attract more guests, and boost your revenue. With actionable insights and proven techniques, these books will give you the knowledge and confidence to turn your real estate investments into profitable, high-performing assets.

Rental Roadblocks: Solving 12 Short- Term Vacation Rental Issues That Impact Your Bottom Line

Facing challenges in your short-term rental journey? _Rental Roadblocks_ identifies 12 common pitfalls that can derail your success, including guest complaints, property damage, and marketing struggles.

Rental Roadblocks provides clear, actionable solutions and expert advice to overcome these obstacles and achieve your rental income goals. Whether you're a seasoned host or just starting out, this book is an essential resource for anyone looking to build a successful and profitable short-term rental business.

Short-Term Stays, Big Profits: Mastering the Vacation Rental Business

Short-Term Stays, Big Profits: Mastering the Vacation Rental Business is a short, straight-forward guide to turning your property into a profitable short-term rental. Whether you're just starting out or an experienced host looking to optimize your business, this book provides a step-by-step roadmap to success.

Short-Term Stays, Big Profits equips you with the knowledge and confidence to build a thriving rental business. Whether you're hosting on Airbnb, Vrbo, or another platform, this guide will help you create a high-demand rental that generates consistent income.

Short-Term Vacation Rental Maintenance Checklist and Planner

A well-maintained short-term vacation rental means happier guests, better reviews, and fewer unexpected issues! Take control of your rental's upkeep and maintenance with this must-have rental maintenance planning tool and checklist.

Short-Term Vacation Rental Turnover Cleaning and Deep Cleaning Checklists

Keep your short-term rental spotless and guest-ready with this comprehensive digital cleaning checklist bundle! Designed for Airbnb, Vrbo, and other vacation rental hosts, this instant download ensures a thorough and efficient cleaning process for every turnover. It also includes a deep cleaning checklist and schedule as well.

You can find more short-term vacation rental tools, templates, and resourcs in our Etsy Shop - Otis Design Boutique!

It's time to pass on your thoughts and show other readers where they can find this book.

Simply by leaving your honest opinion of your purchase on Amazon, you'll show others where they can find books and products they may be interested in.

Thank you for your help!

Scan code to leave a review on Amazon